NUMB TO THIS

Memoir of a Mass Shooting

NUMB TO THIS

Memoir of a Mass Shooting

KINDRA NEELY

Little, Brown and Company
New York Boston

ABOUT THIS BOOK

This book was edited by Andrea Colvin and designed by Megan McLaughlin. The production was supervised by Bernadette Flinn, and the production editor was Lindsay Walter-Greaney. The text was set in Action Figure BB and Din and the display type is Colby Compressed and Nexa.

Little, Brown and Company
Hachette Book Group
1290 Avenue of the Americas, New York, NY 10104
Visit us at LBYR.com

First Edition: October 2022

Little, Brown and Company is a division of Hachette Book Group, Inc.
The Little, Brown name and logo are trademarks of Hachette Book Group, Inc.

The publisher is not responsible for websites (or their content) that are not owned by the publisher.

Library of Congress Cataloging-in-Publication Data
Names: Neely, Kindra, author. | Neely, Kindra, illustrator.
Title: Numb to this: memoir of a mass shooting / Kindra Neely.
Description: First edition. | New York : Little, Brown and Company, 2022. | Audience: Ages 14 & up | Summary: "Author Kindra Neely recounts her journey to healing after surviving a mass shooting during her first year of college." —Provided by publisher.
Identifiers: LCCN 2020041822 | ISBN 9780316462082 (hardcover) | ISBN 9780316462099 (trade paperback) | ISBN 9780316462075 (ebook)
Subjects: LCSH: Neely, Kindra—Comic books, strips, etc. | Victims of violent crimes—Oregon—Roseburg—Biography—Comic books, strips, etc. | School shootings—Oregon—Roseburg—Comic books, strips, etc. | Umpqua Community College (Roseburg, Or.)—Comic books, strips, etc. | Graphic novels.
Classification: LCC HV6250.3.U53 R676 2022 | DDC 362.88/293092 [B]—dc23
LC record available at https://lccn.loc.gov/2020041822

ISBNs: 978-0-316-46208-2 (hardcover), 978-0-316-46209-9 (pbk.), 978-0-316-46207-5 (ebook), 978-0-316-28072-3 (ebook), 978-0-316-28082-2 (ebook)

PRINTED IN CHINA

APS

Hardcover: 10 9 8 7 6 5 4 3 2 1

Paperback: 10 9 8 7 6 5 4 3 2 1

This book is dedicated to those who have been taken by gun violence and to the families, loved ones, and first responders who carry on their memories.

MY MOM AND I MOVED TO OREGON WHEN I WAS 13, BUT BEFORE THAT WE LIVED IN WICHITA FALLS, TEXAS.

MY LIFE IN TEXAS WAS A LOT DIFFERENT FROM MY LIFE IN OREGON.

WE PLAYED IN STORM DITCHES--

2

I WENT TO SCHOOL WITH METAL DETECTORS--

AND POLICE DOGS--

AND OFFICERS.

FIGHT! THERE'S A GIRL WITH A RAZOR!

MOVE! OUT OF THE WAY!

3

ON THE LORD'S DAY, WE WENT TO THE BIG CHURCH--

A PROPER SOUTHERN MEGACHURCH.

WE EVEN HAD ONE OF THOSE TV PASTORS.

WHEN MY MOM WORKED IN THE AIR FORCE, WE LIVED IN THE NICER PART OF THE CITY.

WHEN SHE HAD TO LEAVE BECAUSE OF A DISABILITY, WE ENDED UP MOVING A FEW TIMES.

I WAS TOO YOUNG TO UNDERSTAND, BUT WE KEPT LOSING MONEY.

UNTIL WE ENDED UP ON THE EDGE OF THE CITY LIMIT.

THERE WERE A LOT OF GUNS--

BUT THAT WAS PRETTY NORMAL.

HEY, KID.

HEY.

EVERYBODY CARRIED IN TEXAS.

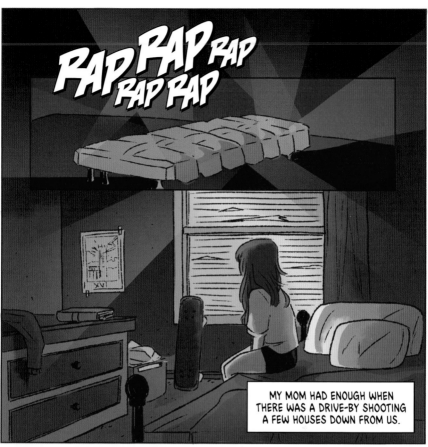

MY MOM HAD ENOUGH WHEN THERE WAS A DRIVE-BY SHOOTING A FEW HOUSES DOWN FROM US.

THAT HOUSE LOOKED LIKE SWISS CHEESE THE NEXT DAY.

SHE SPENT EVERY
LAST CENT TO GET
US AWAY FROM IT--

AND MOVED
US TO HER
HOMETOWN:

ROSEBURG,
OREGON.

I WENT TO THE SAME HIGH SCHOOL SHE DID.

AND I MADE A FRIEND.

THE GIRL SKATES!

A LOT OF FRIENDS.

LIKE CHLOE, WHO LOVED TO DRAW.

CASEY AND I MET IN HOMEROOM. WE BAKED A LOT FOR OUR CLASSMATES.

I MET BRETT DURING PLAY PRACTICE.

WE HUNG OUT AT THE RIVER, INSTEAD OF DITCHES.

THE SCHOOL HAD SECURITY GUARDS--

BUT THEY WERE MOSTLY THERE TO MAKE SURE WE WEREN'T SKIPPING CLASS.

HIGH FIVE, MR. P!

HAVE A GOOD DAY!

WHEN IT CAME TO CHOOSING A COLLEGE--

UCC.

I KNEW EXACTLY WHERE I WANTED TO GO.

YOU KNOW, COMMUNITY COLLEGE IS A GREAT--OH, YOU ACTUALLY WANT TO GO?

I'M 17! I CAN'T GO INTO DEBT IF I DON'T KNOW WHAT I WANT TO DO!

SOME PEOPLE MIGHT THINK IT'S STRANGE, BUT I THINK IT'S THE BEST DECISION I'VE EVER MADE.

IT LED TO MEETING MY BEST FRIEND, JASMINE.

MOST OF MY FRIENDS FROM HIGH SCHOOL STAYED, TOO.

JASMINE FIT RIGHT IN.

JAZZ WINS; HER CARD WAS BEST.

NO WAY! AGAIN?

UCC KEPT PUSHING ME-- NOT JUST TO FIND WHAT I WANTED TO DO, BUT WHO I WANTED TO BE.

TWEEEE

I KNEW I LIKED HELPING PEOPLE AND WAS WILLING TO PUT IN THE WORK TO DO IT PROPERLY.

BAM! ALL BETTER!

IT'S WATERPROOF?

HECK YEAH, ONLY THE BEST.

14

IT'S NOT THAT EVERYTHING WAS PERFECT IN OREGON--

BUT I COULD BE MYSELF--

AND HAVE THE SPACE TO FIGURE OUT WHAT EXACTLY THAT MEANT.

GUN VIOLENCE WASN'T SOMETHING I WAS UNACCUSTOMED TO.

IT JUST WASN'T EXPECTED.

NOT HERE.

17

BRRRING

6:00 AM
THURSDAY, OCT 1st

IS IT BAD THAT I WANT TO SLEEP IN? IT'S ONLY THE FOURTH DAY OF SCHOOL.

NO MORE LATE DRIVES FOR ME.

LET'S DO THIS.

TEETH. CHECK.

DO I NEED TO BRUSH MY HAIR?

EXTRA CLOTHES. CHECK.

CLOSE THE DOOR QUIETLY SO MOM DOESN'T WAKE UP.

KEYS? CHECK.

ALWAYS TAKE THE SCENIC ROUTE.

MY WORK IS ON YOUR DESK, PROFESSOR. I'M OFF TO THE POOL.

GREAT, SEE YOU NEXT CLASS!

JUST RUN.

I JUST NEED A MINUTE.

I JUST NEED TO THINK.

28

SHOULD I FOLLOW HER?

I DON'T FEEL RIGHT.

WAIT, CARA, KALEB!

32

THEY COULD GET HURT STANDING AROUND LIKE THAT, AND CARA AND KALEB ARE ATHLETES.

I'M GOING BACK.

WHAT? NO!

YEAH, I DON'T THINK I CAN KEEP UP WITH YOU GUYS.

AND THEY DON'T KNOW WHAT'S HAPPENING.

IT'LL BE OK.

SHE'S RIGHT THERE; SHE SAID SOMEONE WAS ON CAMPUS.

SO, WHAT IS HAPPENING?

YEAH, THERE'S A SHOOTER, DOWN BY SNYDER.

EVERYONE, INSIDE RIGHT NOW!

MY FRIENDS WERE IN THE LIBRARY, BUT I DON'T KNOW IF HE WAS THERE OR NOT.

OK. LET ME MAKE A PHONE CALL. EVERYONE, JUST SIT DOWN AND WE'LL FIGURE THIS OUT.

CLICK

SHOULD I CALL SOMEONE?

37

THE EMERGENCY-ALERT SYSTEM FAILED.

UGH, COMMUNITY COLLEGE.

I DON'T THINK THEY REALIZE THAT PEOPLE ARE REALLY HURT.

UH-HUH, OK.

IT'S OVER.

YOU GUYS CAN GO; JUST DON'T GO DOWN TOWARD SNYDER.

OVER? WHAT DOES THAT EVEN MEAN?

GO?

GO WHERE?

I CAN'T GET TO MY CAR; IT'S RIGHT NEXT TO SNYDER.

IF HE'S LETTING US OUT, DOES THAT MEAN IT WASN'T VERY SERIOUS? IS THAT LADY OK, THEN?

40

42

43

UM, THERE WAS A SHOOTING.

WHAT? WHAT'S GOING ON? WHERE ARE YOU?

PEOPLE-- I THINK A LOT OF PEOPLE ARE REALLY HURT, MOM.

I HEARD A LADY SAY 20 ARE DEAD.

OK, OK, UM, ARE YOU WITH ANYONE? CAN YOU SEE YOUR FRIENDS?

I'M AT THE POOL WITH PEOPLE, BUT NO, I'M--MY FRIENDS AREN'T HERE. I'M ALONE.

WE'RE SWITCHING ROOMS TO BE SAFER, BUT THE POLICE ALREADY GOT THE GUY, I THINK.

AND WHAT ABOUT YOUR CAR? CAN YOU COME HOME?

IT'S BY WHERE IT HAPPENED. I DON'T THINK WE'RE ALLOWED TO LEAVE.

HEY, I THINK I SEE MY FRIEND JOSH.

OK, IT LOOKS LIKE THEY ARE GOING TO EVACUATE YOU GUYS TO THE FAIRGROUNDS. I'M GOING TO LET YOU GO AND HEAD OVER THERE. JUST CALL IF YOU HEAR ANYTHING, OK?

OK.

KINDRA!

WE WAITED FOR THREE HOURS.

SOME PEOPLE PRAYED.

BUT MOSTLY WE JUST SAT IN SILENCE AND SLOWLY PIECED TOGETHER WHAT WAS HAPPENING OUTSIDE.

ONE OF THE FIRST RESPONDERS HAD WALKED INTO THE CLASSROOM WHERE IT HAPPENED TO FIND HIS SON DEAD.

SOMEONE FOUND THE HATEFUL RANTS THE SHOOTER HAD POSTED.

MEANWHILE, THE PRESS WAS QUESTIONING JOSH. I GUESS BECAUSE HE WAS THE STUDENT BODY PRESIDENT AND THEY FOUND HIS PROFILE.

48

THE POLICE HAD BEEN CLEARING THE CLASSROOMS ONE BY ONE, AND WE WERE THE VERY LAST TO BE EVACUATED.

BANG

EVERYBODY, SHOW US YOUR HANDS!

ANYONE HURT? NO?

OK, LISTEN, LEAVE YOUR BACKPACKS IF YOU CAN, AND KEEP YOUR HANDS ABOVE YOUR HEAD AT ALL TIMES. WE NEED YOU TO LINE UP SINGLE FILE.

WE NEED TO PAT YOU DOWN, THEN WE'LL GET YOU GUYS OUT TO THE FAIRGROUNDS, OK?

49

THIS
FEELS LIKE
A MOVIE.

HEY, IT'S OK TO PUT YOUR HANDS DOWN. THE BUS IS RIGHT OVER THERE.

THE COLLEGE HAS ONE ROAD IN AND OUT. AND IT WAS LINED WITH POLICE AND STATE TROOPER CARS.

DURING SUMMER YOU COULD PARK YOUR CAR AT THE HIGH SCHOOL AND TAKE A BUS TO THE FAIRGROUNDS. THIS FELT LIKE A REALLY MESSED-UP VERSION OF THAT. IT WAS FAMILIAR, BUT WRONG.

MOM!

OPEN HOUSE, LIKE ALWAYS. FEEL FREE TO COME IF YOU NEED A BREATHER.

EVERYONE HAD BEEN WAITING.

WHERE WERE YOU GUYS?

HERE, NONE OF US HAD CLASSES THIS MORNING.

WHY DON'T WE HEAD BACK TO THE HOUSE?

CHLOE, WE'RE LEAVING.

OK, WE'LL SEE YOU LATER.

BY THE TIME WE REACHED THE CAR--

A PICTURE OF JOSH AND ME HUGGING HAD BEEN POSTED BY A NATIONAL NEWSPAPER.

OREGON CAMPUS SHOOTING

I FELT SO VIOLATED. PEOPLE WERE GOING TO MAKE THEIR OWN ASSUMPTIONS ABOUT THE PEOPLE IN THE PHOTO WITHOUT EVER KNOWING HOW WE ACTUALLY FELT OR WHAT IT WAS LIKE.

THE NATION WAS WATCHING US WHILE WE WERE MOST VULNERABLE, BUT IT FELT LIKE WE WERE ENTERTAINMENT.

I HADN'T EVEN BEEN HOME YET.

WHEN WE GOT HOME, THE TV WAS STILL ON.

PRESIDENT OBAMA WAS ADDRESSING THE SITUATION.

SOMEHOW, THIS HAS BECOME ROUTINE.

THAT NIGHT, WE WENT TO THE PARK TO ATTEND A VIGIL.

NORMALLY, WE'D COME HERE TO SEE A CONCERT OR THE FIREWORKS SHOW DURING THE FOURTH OF JULY.

SEEING IT CROWDED WAS NORMAL, BUT THE REASON WAS NOT.

COME ON, SWEETIE. THIS WAY.

HERE, WE'VE GOT CANDLES.

OH, THANK YOU.

THERE WERE SEVERAL SPEAKERS.

I THINK THEY WERE TRYING TO BE SYMPATHETIC, BUT IT FELT FORCED.

YOU CAN'T REALLY BE HOPEFUL OR RESILIENT IF YOU HAVEN'T PROCESSED THAT WHAT YOU'VE BEEN THROUGH THREATENS THOSE FEELINGS.

THE MEDIA WERE TOO DISTRACTING.

THE SHOOTER WAS DEAD AND WOULD NEVER BE HELD ACCOUNTABLE FOR HIS ACTIONS. BUT REPORTERS COULD.

SHOVING CAMERAS AND MICROPHONES IN OUR FACES WAS TOO MUCH TOO SOON.

IT FELT LIKE WE WERE ON DISPLAY, LIKE WE WERE BEING TAKEN ADVANTAGE OF.

IT FELT LIKE THEY CARED MORE ABOUT THEIR CAREERS THAN THE PEOPLE WHO WERE RIGHT IN FRONT OF THEM.

SORRY, WHO ARE THOSE FLOWERS FOR?

HE'S NOT ASKING BECAUSE HE CARES.

HE'S SMILING BECAUSE THEY DON'T KNOW THE NAMES OF ALL THE VICTIMS.

AND HE THINKS I'M ABOUT TO GIVE HIM A NAME THAT THE OTHERS DON'T HAVE.

JUST FOR THOSE THAT WE LOST.

UH, OK.

LET'S JUST GO.

THE NEXT MORNING WAS WORSE.

MY PICTURE WAS IN THE PAPER AGAIN.

HEY, KINDRA, COULD YOU CHECK ON EMERSON? HE SAYS HE'S FINE, BUT I THINK HE'D TALK TO YOU.

YEAH, OF COURSE.

HEY, I KNOW WE HAVEN'T TALKED IN A WHILE, BUT I WANTED TO SEE HOW YOU ARE.

PEOPLE WERE DEALING WITH THE AWKWARDNESS IN DIFFERENT WAYS.

WE COULD SUE THE SCHOOL FOR THE ALARM SYSTEM FAILING.

YEAH, MY LIFE COULD HAVE BEEN TAKEN!

THEY'RE SO LOUD.

HEY, CAN YOU GUYS TALK ABOUT THAT SOMEWHERE ELSE? YOU'RE MAKING PEOPLE REALLY UNCOMFORTABLE.

NO, BECAUSE FREEDOM OF SPEECH!

MIND YOUR OWN BUSINESS.

74

I WAS THINKING WE HAVE THAT SPACE OUTSIDE, AND WHY NOT MAKE IT A MEMORIAL?

I WAS WONDERING IF YOU WANTED TO COME UP WITH SOME DESIGNS?

ME?

WOW, UM, YES.

DID YOU HAVE ANYTHING SPECIFIC IN MIND?

ACTUALLY, YES. YOU KNOW GEORGE? HE WAS VERY CLOSE TO LARRY, THE PROFESSOR WHO PASSED.

"LARRY LIKED TO GO FLY-FISHING, AND HE HAD NEVER SEEN A RED DRAGONFLY UNTIL JUST THE OTHER DAY. HE WAS JUST REALLY EXCITED TO TELL GEORGE THAT HE HAD SEEN ONE RIGHT BEFORE HE WENT TO TEACH CLASS.

THIS IS GREAT. LET'S GO LOOK AT SOME TILE COLORS.

ART JUST FELT RIGHT. IT WAS A PRODUCTIVE AND CONSTRUCTIVE WAY TO EXPRESS MY FEELINGS. IT GAVE ME A PLACE TO THINK ABOUT THE...THE *INCIDENT* WITHOUT STEWING IN NEGATIVITY.

WHEN THE SUPPLIES CAME IN, I SPENT HOURS CAREFULLY DESIGNING THE DRAGONFLIES THAT REPRESENTED THE STUDENTS AND PROFESSOR WHO PASSED.

EACH ONE HAD A UNIQUE DESIGN.

FOR THE FIREFIGHTER'S SON, I PUT AN X DESIGN ON THE BODY TO MIMIC THE SUSPENDERS THEY WEAR UNDER THEIR JACKETS.

ONCE THE DRAGONFLIES WERE UP, IT BECAME MORE OF A COMMUNITY PROJECT. IT WAS NICE TO INVITE OTHERS TO SHARE A SAFE PLACE AND COLLABORATE ON A TASK THAT HELPED THEM MOVE FORWARD.

I WAS JUST GLAD I GOT TO CONTRIBUTE SOMETHING MEANINGFUL.

AND IT HELPED ME DECIDE THAT ART WAS THE RIGHT PLACE FOR ME.

I'M HOME.

GOOD DAY, HONEY?

YEAH, ACTUALLY.

HEY, KITTY.

NOW, LET'S SEE...

SEARCH: ART SCHOOLS

HMM, NONE OF THESE ARE CLICKING. MARYLAND? THAT'S TOO COLD. MAYBE I SHOULD JUST LOOK AT OREGON SCHOOLS.

WHAT'S THAT SCHOOL THAT GIRL ON INSTAGRAM GOES TO?

SCAD

UNIVERSITY FOR CREATIVE CARE

SCAD? WOW, THIS LOOKS GREAT. GEORGIA IS SO FAR AWAY, THOUGH.

I'LL JUST APPLY. IT'S NOT LIKE I HAVE TO GO.

IMAGINE YOURSELF HERE

APPLY

86

ARE YOU GOING TO TELL BRETT? HE'S GOING TO FLIP. HE'S ALREADY GONE TO OREGON STATE.

NO, THERE'S NOTHING TO TELL. I MIGHT STILL JOIN HIM AND THE BOYS NEXT FALL.

GIVE HER A DAY; SHE'S ALWAYS CHANGING HER MAJOR ANYWAY.

HAHAHA, YESH.

I KNOW SHE'S JOKING, SO WHY AM I SO IRRITATED?

DO YOU GUYS WANT TO HAVE A GAME NIGHT THIS WEEKEND?

SURE!

YES, MAYBE.

DON'T SAY YES IF YOU'RE GONNA BAIL OR COMPLAIN THE WHOLE TIME.

I WANT TO STOP. I REALLY DO.

I MIGHT TAKE A LONG TIME TO DECIDE WHAT TO DO, BUT AT LEAST I DO WHAT I SAY I'M GOING TO DO.

I'M NOT REALLY UPSET THAT SHE DOESN'T SHOW UP. IT'S JUST THAT I KEEP TRYING TO REACH OUT, AND WHEN SHE DOESN'T SHOW, IT FEELS LIKE I'M NOT IMPORTANT.

THE SHOOTING SEEMED TO HIGHLIGHT SOME ISSUES IN MY FRIENDSHIPS THAT HAD BEEN THERE FOR A WHILE.

IT JUST FEELS LIKE THEY DON'T REALLY LISTEN TO ME.

THERE ARE WORSE PEOPLE OUT THERE, KINDRA.

DUDE, WHAT ARE YOU EVEN TALKING ABOUT?

WHAT? I WASN'T SAYING THEY WERE A BAD PERSON. YOU CAN HAVE A CONFLICT WITH SOMEONE WITHOUT RAGGING ON THEM.

MAINLY, HOW WE COMMUNICATED.

I TOLD YOU, LIKE, THREE TIMES THAT I GET CARSICK!

THAT'S NOT MY FAULT!

HA! YOU SUCK!

BRETT, CHILL. IT'S A GAME.

WE GET IT: YOU'RE STRONG AND INDEPENDENT!

IT WAS A JOKE! I DIDN'T NEED YOUR HELP GETTING OVER THAT TREE!

SOMETIMES YOUR FRIENDS JUST WANT TO HELP YOU!

BUT I DIDN'T *NEED* HELP WITH THAT!

WOW, YEAH, JUST WALK AWAY INSTEAD OF TALKING LIKE AN ADULT!

WELL, I DIDN'T KNOW!

OH MY GOD, WHY CAN'T YOU JUST LISTEN TO ME FOR ONCE?

WHEN I WAS ACCEPTED TO ART SCHOOL, IT WASN'T THAT HARD TO DECIDE TO LEAVE.

WE ARE PLEASED TO INFORM ACCEPTANCE TO SCAD.

I LOVED MY HOME.

IT'S JUST EVERYTHING FELT WRONG. I FELT WRONG.

BRETT

HEY, I GOT INTO THIS SCHOOL IN GEORGIA, AND I'M GOING.

WHAT? WHAT ABOUT OREGON STATE?

I DON'T WANT THAT ANYMORE.

YOU NEVER TAKE TIME FOR ANYONE, AND YOU'RE SO *JUDGMENTAL!* I DON'T WANT TO BE FRIENDS ANYMORE!

WELL, *FINE!* I DON'T WANT TO BE FRIENDS, EITHER!

IT FELT LIKE I WAS LOSING EVERYTHING I LOVED ABOUT ROSEBURG.

I TRIED TO KEEP THE ANGER UNDER CONTROL.

I MEAN, IN THE MOMENT, IT FELT GOOD TO BICKER ABOUT STUPID THINGS.

BUT WHEN I LOOKED IN THE MIRROR, IT DIDN'T LOOK LIKE ME.

ALMOST READY?

YEAH.

IF I WAS BEING HONEST, I HADN'T FELT LIKE MYSELF IN A WHILE.

GRADUATION
1PM-3PM
→
FOOD AND
DRINKS @
COMPASS
AFTERWARDS

GRADUATION IS SUPPOSED TO BE CHEERFUL, BUT I JUST FEEL AWFUL.

I FEEL ACCOMPLISHED, BUT I FEEL LIKE I SHOULD BE HAPPIER.

AND I'M JUST NOT.

PST! KINDRA!

KINDRA, YOUR NAME IS ON THE PLAQUE! YOU GOT THE AWARD!

WOW, WHAT?

THE WINNER OF THE HARRY JACOBY AWARD IS A PERSON WHO SHOWS EXCELLENCE IN SCHOOL AND COMMUNITY.

THIS YEAR'S WINNER IS KINDRA NEELY!

A FEW OF US HAD BEEN NOMINATED EARLIER IN THE YEAR, BUT I HONESTLY DIDN'T THINK I WOULD WIN.

JUST TRY NOT TO FALL ON YOUR FACE IN FRONT OF YOUR WHOLE SCHOOL.

ONE HOUR EARLIER.

HEY, KINDRA, YOU KNOW WE HAVE TO GIVE A SPEECH IF WE WIN, RIGHT?

JOSH WAS ULTRADECORATED WITH ALL THE ACCOMPLISHMENTS HE'D ACHIEVED.

WHILE I WAS THE LEAST DECORATED OF THE FINAL NOMINEES.

THAT'S GONNA SUCK FOR WHOEVER WINS.

WOW, UM, THANK YOU.

THANK YOU.

THIS FEELS LIKE SOMETHING I WOULD SAY.

AND I DO BELIEVE IT.

BUT IT ALSO FEELS LIKE I'M JUST SAYING WHAT I NEED TO SAY...

...TO SEEM NORMAL.

GOOD SPEECH, HONEY.

THANKS.

MY BIRTHDAY WAS A FEW DAYS AFTER GRADUATION.

YAY, I'M 20.

UGH.

I SHOULD PUT ON SOME CLOTHES.

IT FELT LIKE NO PART OF MY LIFE WAS GOING UNTOUCHED.

FEAR WAS MAKING IT IMPOSSIBLE TO MAKE NEW, HAPPY MEMORIES.

THIS WAS EVERYWHERE.

IT'S MY BIRTHDAY.

JUNE 13TH

JASMINE:
HAPPY BIRTHDAY!

AND FOR THE FIRST TIME, I DON'T REALLY SEE A POINT IN HAVING ANOTHER.

IT WAS LIKE THAT THE ENTIRE SUMMER.

IT JUST KEPT FESTERING--

THIS FEELING OF POINTLESSNESS.

UNTIL I
JUST DIDN'T FEEL
ANYTHING--

AND IT DIDN'T
MATTER.

107

THIS WAS NOT ONE OF THOSE TIMES.

I JUST DIDN'T SEE THE POINT IN TRYING ANYMORE.

SHOOTINGS WERE JUST GOING TO KEEP HAPPENING.

BOOM. FRIES AND THE BEST SAUCE THIS SIDE OF THE SAFARI.

YES! THANKS!

I WISH YOU COULD STAY AND WORK THE OFF-SEASON, BUT ART SCHOOL SOUNDS FUN.

PEOPLE ASSUME THAT PEOPLE WHO ARE SUICIDAL ACT DIFFERENTLY. THEY DON'T MAKE PLANS.

SOMETIMES THEY DON'T EVEN KNOW THEY WANT TO END THEIR LIFE--

BYE! THANKS FOR YOUR PATIENCE. ENJOY THE PARK!

BYE, MISS LADY!

SO THERE ARE NO SIGNS.

I'M NOT GIVING YOU ANY MORE FOOD. NICE TRY.

111

IT WAS A
MOMENT OF
APATHY.

I JUST DIDN'T FEEL LIKE TURNING OFF THE CAR.

BZZT
BZZT

JUST SIT AND
ENJOY THE
SILENCE.

HMM?

I'VE NEVER REALLY TOLD YOU ABOUT LEXA.

YOUR FRIEND FROM BEFORE WE MET?

YEAH, WE WERE REALLY CLOSE.

"WE GREW UP TOGETHER.

"BUT IN HIGH SCHOOL, SHE WAS DEPRESSED.

"SHE WAS GOING THROUGH A ROUGH TIME.

"I TRIED TO HELP HER, BUT...

"...SHE KILLED HERSELF.

"AND IT HURT. SO BAD.

"AND FOR SO LONG.

"AND IT STILL HURTS.

"EVERY. SINGLE. DAY.

"IT'S BEEN YEARS, KINDRA.

"I STILL MISS HER.

"AND I HAVEN'T FELT THAT CLOSE TO ANYONE SINCE THEN--

"EXCEPT FOR YOU."

123

YEAH, THAT SOUNDS AMAZING.

JUST, UM, JUST IN A LITTLE BIT. I NEED TO SHOWER.

I FEEL GROSS.

WELL, YOU DO WORK AT A ZOO.

HEY, JAZZ--

THANKS FOR INVITING ME OUT.

OF COURSE! ARE YOU DOING OK?

I WANTED TO TELL HER--

YEAH, OF COURSE.

BUT EVERYONE KEPT TELLING ME HOW STRONG I WAS.

AND I DIDN'T WANT TO DISAPPOINT THEM.

OK, WELL, TEXT ME WHEN YOU'RE READY.

I'M NOT
STRONG; LOOK
AT WHAT I'VE
DONE.

126

JOSH AND CHLOE'S GETTING MARRIED FELT LIKE AN EMOTIONAL TRIUMPH.

IT WAS NICE SEEING TWO PEOPLE BELIEVE IN A FUTURE TOGETHER.

I NEED TO LEAVE SOON SO I CAN FINISH PACKING TONIGHT, BUT I WISH THIS COULD LAST A LITTLE LONGER.

MAYBE IT'S ENOUGH RIGHT NOW TO LIVE SO THAT I DON'T MESS UP OTHER PEOPLE'S MOMENTS. I COULD HAVE HURT A LOT OF PEOPLE. I'M NOT HAPPY, BUT I DON'T WANT OTHERS TO BE UNHAPPY, AND MAYBE THAT'S A START TO GETTING BETTER.

128

I LEFT BEFORE CHLOE THREW THE BOUQUET.

IT FELT SILLY TO CARE ABOUT A WEDDING SUPERSTITION IF I STILL DIDN'T SEE MUCH OF A FUTURE.

JASMINE AND BRETT WERE WAITING TO SEE ME OFF TO GEORGIA.

HEY! GO GET CHANGED! LET'S LIGHT OFF SOME FIREWORKS BEFORE YOU LEAVE!

SOUNDS FUN.

EH, WE'LL BE CAREFUL.

THIS IS A GOOD, ROCKY SPOT.

YEAH, THE TREES ARE FAR BACK.

ONLY ONE. LET'S DO THIS.

IT WAS A MOMENT I WAS GLAD I DIDN'T MISS.

AND MAYBE THAT WAS ENOUGH FOR NOW.

I'LL JUST KEEP WAITING FOR MOMENTS LIKE THESE.

WE DROVE ALL THE WAY TO GEORGIA.

I DON'T GET IT. IT'S JUST A BIG BEAN.

135

137

NEAT.

STRANGE, THERE'S ONLY ONE DOOR.

IT'S KIND OF CRAMPED IN HERE.

I FEEL LIKE IT'S HARD TO BREATHE.

WHAT IF SOMETHING HAPPENS AGAIN AND I CAN'T GET OUT?

WOOMPF WOOMPF WOOMPF

A HELICOPTER.

WOW, THEY'RE SO CLOSE!

141

SOMEHOW, WE'VE BECOME NUMB TO THIS.

HEY, KIDDO. WOW, MARINE ONE!

WHAT?

OH, UH, YEAH.

LITTLE CROWDED IN THERE?

YEAH.

HEY, DO YOU REMEMBER WHEN OBAMA CAME TO ROSEBURG?

YEAH, AND ALL THOSE DUMB PEOPLE FROM OUT OF TOWN CAME TO PROTEST.

PFT, TELL ME HOW YOU REALLY FEEL, MOM.

WELL, I'M JUST SAYING! HE CAME TO SEE THE FAMILIES AND THE INJURED.

NO ONE ELSE HAD ANY RIGHT TO SAY IF HE SHOULD BE THERE OR NOT. THEY DON'T SPEAK FOR US.

HMM, IT'S LIKE "THOUGHTS AND PRAYERS" IS TOO APATHETIC, BUT COMING TO OUR TOWN IS TOO MUCH. IT MADE THEM FEEL BETTER, BUT IT WASN'T WHAT WAS BEST FOR US.

IT'S LIKE PEOPLE JUST WANT TO TALK FOR US OR AT US.

BUT NO ONE SEEMS TO BE LISTENING.

HOW ARE WE SUPPOSED TO GET BETTER IF WE CAN'T LISTEN TO THOSE WHO ARE DIRECTLY INVOLVED?

IT FEELS LIKE PEOPLE JUST WANT TO ARGUE TALKING POINTS, BUT NO ONE WANTS TO GET BETTER.

145

LOOKS LIKE THEY'RE ALREADY MOVED IN.

THAT MUST BE MY SIDE.

TIME TO DECORATE!

AND PLUGGING--

AND HANGING--

AND FLOOFING--

148

AND DONE!

MWAH! BEAUTIFUL! I AM OFFICIALLY A DUMB COLLEGE GIRL.

IS THAT THE FRONT DOOR? I WONDER IF IT'S MY ROOMIE.

HELLO?

I LOVE THEM, AND I WILL DIE FOR THEM.

HI THERE, NICE TO MEET YOU. I'M KINDRA'S MOM.

HI. I'M RADHII.

OK, BE COOL, YOU HAVE TO LIVE WITH THIS PERSON FOR A WHOLE YEAR.

HI, I'M KINDRA.

HI, I'M RADHII.

YEAH, IT WAS A LITTLE CONCERNING WHEN THE TAXI DRIVER TOLD US TO BE CAREFUL BECAUSE THE SOUTH ISN'T ALWAYS WELCOMING TO MUSLIMS.

SOME PLACES ARE LIKE THAT--

BUT SAVANNAH SHOULD BE OK. THEY HAVE A LOT OF INTERNATIONAL STUDENTS BECAUSE OF THE SCHOOL.

BUT IF ANYONE GIVES YOU TROUBLE, I GOT YOUR BACK.

HA! THANKS.

RADHII AND I GOT CLOSE REALLY QUICKLY.

B

THEY WERE EASY TO TALK TO--

BUT IT WAS HARD TO TELL THEM THAT THE ANNIVERSARY WAS COMING UP.

SO I MIGHT BE A LITTLE WEIRD IN A WEEK OR SO.

I JUST DON'T REALLY KNOW WHAT TO EXPECT.

HEY, IT'S OK. JUST LET ME KNOW WHAT YOU WANT, WHEN YOU KNOW IT.

I THINK WE WON THE RANDOMLY ASSIGNED ROOMMATE LOTTERY.

SOME OF MY CLASSMATES HAVE BEEN SAYING SOME REALLY INSENSITIVE STUFF.

I DON'T THINK THEY REALIZE.

IF ANYONE SAYS ANYTHING BAD TO YOU, I'LL TOTALLY BEAT THEM UP.

PFFTT, KINDRA!

I MAY BE AN OREGON GIRL NOW--

BUT I WAS BORN IN TEXAS. AND EVERYBODY KNOWS, YOU DON'T MESS WITH TEXAS.

157

CRITIQUE DAY.

SHOULD BE EASY...

...AND A NICE DISTRACTION.

THAT WAS A LOUD ONE. PROBABLY JUST A TAILPIPE.

OH NO, DON'T FREAK OUT.

NOT HERE.

EH, IT'S BREAK TIME ANYWAY. BE BACK IN 15.

THANK GOD.

EXCUSE ME.

JUST BREATHE, JUST BREATHE.

PLEASE STOP, PLEASE.

DON'T LOOK AT ME.

PLEASE DON'T TAKE MY PICTURE.

I WANT OUT. I WANT OUT OF MY HEAD!

DON'T THINK. DON'T THINK ABOUT THAT.

I WANT OUT.

EVERYTHING FEELS QUIET NOW.

HOW LONG HAVE I BEEN IN HERE?

FORTY-FIVE MINUTES? I KNOW I SHOULD BE UPSET. I **WAS** SO UPSET.

I FEEL SO NUMB RIGHT NOW.

DO I TELL SOMEONE?

AND SAY WHAT? I FREAKED OUT, BUT NOW I CAN'T REMEMBER WHY I WAS SO UPSET?

THAT SOUNDS CRAZY.

NO, THIS IS THE WAY THINGS ARE NOW. I JUST HAVE TO DEAL.

OCTOBER 1, 2016:
THE FIRST
ANNIVERSARY.

A CHARITY RUN WAS PUT TOGETHER FOR THE ANNIVERSARY.

GREAT, THAT MEANS IT'S 10 IN OREGON AND THEY'RE STARTING THE RUN.

I COULDN'T THINK OF A BETTER WAY TO SPEND THE ANNIVERSARY.

IT WAS THE ONLY THING THAT MADE ME FEEL CONNECTED, SINCE I WAS SO FAR AWAY.

I KNOW THIS IS GOOD--

BUT IT SUCKS THAT I'M ALONE.

HUH, ANOTHER SCAD BUILDING. THERE ARE SO MANY.

WONDER WHAT THEY DO IN HAYMENS HALL?

I'LL HAVE TO CHECK IT OUT LATER.

BAY

THESE STAIRS ARE A DEATH TRAP.

SO MAYBE THIS ISN'T THE IDEAL WAY TO SPEND THE ANNIVERSARY.

RUNNING, ALONE.

MAYBE I SHOULD JUST BE GRATEFUL THAT I'M NOT LOCKED IN A CLASSROOM THIS TIME.

169

RADHII, YOU UP? DID YOU CALL FOR ME?

I'M SORRY!

WHAT?

HEY, HEY, IT'S OK. JUST TELL ME WHAT'S GOING ON.

I'M SO SORRY.

ALL MY FAMILY IS WORRIED SOMETHING IS GOING TO HAPPEN TO ME BECAUSE OF THE ELECTION.

I WOKE UP TO A DOZEN MESSAGES OF THEM SAYING IT'S OK TO PRETEND I'M NOT MUSLIM. THAT IT'S OK FOR MY SAFETY.

AM I GOING TO HAVE TO HIDE WHO I AM? I ALREADY DON'T WEAR A HIJAB!

WHAT CLASSES DO YOU HAVE TOMORROW? I'LL WALK YOU.

NO, I DON'T WANT TO BURDEN YOU.

IT'S NO BURDEN. I DON'T WANT YOU TO FEEL UNSAFE.

IT'S OK. I THINK IT WAS JUST REALLY OVERWHELMING WITH ALL THE MESSAGES.

YOU DON'T HAVE TO APOLOGIZE AT ALL.

WE'LL GET THROUGH THIS.

WE MADE IT THROUGH THE YEAR ALL RIGHT.

RADHII SPENT WINTER BREAK WITH ME IN OREGON.

I GOT RAINED ON A LOT IN SAVANNAH, WHICH I LOVED.

BUT I ALSO GOT SICK A LOT.

BUT WE FINISHED STRONG--

AND WERE EXCITED TO LIVE TOGETHER THE NEXT YEAR.

BUT FIRST, I GOT TO GO HOME FOR THE SUMMER.

KINDRA!

JAZZY!

I MISSED YOU!

I MISSED YOU, TOO!

LET'S GO GET SUSHI.

YEAH, LET'S DO THAT.

SEEING JAZZ MAKES ME FEEL SO HAPPY. IT REMINDS ME OF HOW MUCH I LOVE HOME.

BUT WHILE I'M IN SAVANNAH, IT'S EASY TO REMEMBER AND MISS ONLY THE GOOD THINGS.

NOW THAT I'M BACK, ALL THE BAD MEMORIES ARE MIXED IN.

IT'S HARD TO REALLY ENJOY MYSELF.

HURRY UP, I'M STARVING!

COMING!

DUDE, I'M SO BORED.

SAME.

IT FEELS WEIRD HAVING THE SUMMER OFF.

YEAH, WITH HOW CRAZY THE SCHOOL YEAR HAS BEEN, IT FEELS LIKE CHEATING.

UGH. LET'S JUST WATCH ANOTHER MOVIE.

IT'S NICE TO BE HOME, THOUGH.

"I MISSED THE MOUNTAINS--

"AND THE RIVER--

"AND THE FIREWORKS SHOW."

I'M NERVOUS ABOUT SPENDING THE ANNIVERSARY ALONE AGAIN.

ARE YOU GOING TO DO THE CHARITY RUN AGAIN?

YEAH, PROBABLY.

I WISH I COULD BE WITH YOU GUYS, THOUGH.

WE CAN ALWAYS CALL.

WHEN'S YOUR FLIGHT?

A FEW DAYS.

IT'LL BE OK.

KNOCK
KNOCK

WHAT ARE YOU BUILDING?

IT'S A TOY SHIP.

OH, FOR DESIGN CLASS?

YEAH.

"*PETER PAN* WAS ONE OF MY FAVORITE STORIES."

I THOUGHT BEING A KID FOREVER AND GETTING TO HANG OUT WITH YOUR FRIENDS WAS A PRETTY SWEET DEAL.

BUT I DIDN'T HAVE A LOT OF FRIENDS BEFORE OREGON.

THAT'S WHY IT'S SO SPECIAL TO ME.

AND WHY THE SHOOTING FELT SO-- VIOLATING.

WHAT WERE YOU PLAYING EARLIER? IT SOUNDED REALLY FUN.

OH, I THINK I KNOW.

ARE YOU GONNA BE OK?

YEAH. IT'S JUST A WEIRD DAY.

KEEPING BUSY HELPED TAKE MY MIND OFF IT FOR A WHILE.

BUT I COULDN'T SHAKE THAT I WAS WAITING FOR SOMETHING BAD TO HAPPEN AGAIN.

MY THOUGHTS WERE RACING.

I JUST WANTED MY HEAD TO BE QUIET.

BUT I JUST SLIPPED BACK INTO THAT DAY LIKE IT WAS HAPPENING ALL OVER AGAIN.

WHAT?

NO NO NO
NO. I DON'T
WANT TO THINK
ABOUT THIS.

I JUST WANT A BREAK.

MOM? I JUST WANTED TO LET YOU KNOW I'M OK.

HEY! GET INSIDE RIGHT NOW!

I'M TRYING! SHE WON'T LET ME IN.

JOSH. BREATHE IN THROUGH YOUR NOSE AND OUT THROUGH YOUR MOUTH. WE'RE OK.

BUT THAT'S NOT REALLY TRUE. WE'RE ALIVE, BUT WE'RE NOT REALLY OK.

I SAID I DON'T WANT TO THINK ABOUT THIS ANYMORE!

IT'S FINE.
THIS IS FINE.
I'M FINE.

UGH!

BZZT

BZZT

GREAT. WHO'S
CALLING ME
RIGHT NOW?
IT'S SO LATE.

BZZT

I TRIED TO GO TO CLASS THE NEXT DAY.

BUT I MADE IT THROUGH ONLY ONE.

WHAM

WHY AM I CRYING? NOTHING HAPPENED. NOTHING.

FEAR HAD COMPLETELY TAKEN CONTROL.

IT STARTED AS A VICIOUS CYCLE.

SOMETHING WOULD SCARE ME. IT DIDN'T EVEN HAVE TO BE RELATED TO SHOOTINGS.

I'D GET ANGRY--

THEN SICK--

AND COLD--

UNTIL I THREW UP.

I'D HAVE A COMPLETE EMOTIONAL BREAKDOWN.

IT WOULD STOP SUDDENLY, AND I'D BE CONFUSED AND SPACEY.

I'D TRY TO SLEEP, BECAUSE I WAS ALWAYS EXHAUSTED AFTERWARD, BUT I COULDN'T, BECAUSE THE NIGHTMARES WERE MUCH WORSE.

IT FELT LIKE I KEPT RUNNING INTO DANGER EVERYWHERE I WENT

WEIRD, IT WAS SO CROWDED A FEW MINUTES AGO.

OH, PEOPLE!

HEY, UM. HI, SORRY.

UM, SORRY. WHAT'S GOING ON?

THERE'S A BOMB THREAT; WE NEED TO HEAD OUTSIDE.

SOMETIMES I FELT LIKE IT WAS MY FAULT BAD THINGS WERE HAPPENING. LIKE I WAS BAD LUCK, BECAUSE IT SEEMED TO HAPPEN EVERYWHERE I WENT.

I SHOULD CALL MOM, RIGHT?

UM, HEY, MOM. UM, I GUESS I'M JUST CALLING TO TELL YOU I'M OK AGAIN.

THERE'S A BOMB THREAT AT THE STATION.

WHAT? ARE YOU IN DC?

YEAH, THEY HAVE US OUTSIDE RIGHT NOW.

I JOINED THE SEQUENTIAL-ART DEPARTMENT DURING WINTER QUARTER.

PEPPERMINT TEA AND PEPPER-MINTS. NOT THE MOST NUTRITIOUS BREAKFAST, BUT MY STOMACH IS STILL UPSET FROM LAST NIGHT'S PANIC ATTACK. I REALLY NEED TO GET THOSE UNDER CONTROL.

BZZT

LITTLE EARLY FOR A PHONE CALL--

NEWS 4 U!

NOPE!

I JUST HAVE TO MAKE IT THROUGH CLASS.

JUST A FEW HOURS, AND MAYBE I'LL BE ABLE TO SLEEP WHEN I GET HOME.

AWW, QUILL LOOKS A LITTLE SPIFFY TODAY. I WONDER IF THEY HAVE A VALENTINE?

I DIDN'T REALLY THINK THEY'D BE INTO VALENTINE'S DAY.

I SHOULD TELL THEM THEY LOOK NICE.

OH NO, ARE THEY LOOKING AT ME?

I HAVEN'T PRACTICED HOW TO TELL THEM THEY LOOK NICE! THEY THINK I'M CREEPY! I'VE JUST BEEN STARING!

HEY, EVERYBODY, TIME TO LEARN ABOUT HORROR COMICS!

OH, THANK GOD.

USING ROUGH INKING CAN HELP ADD ATMOSPHERE!

ALL RIGHT, LET'S TAKE A BREAK!

OH, QUILL TOOK OFF PRETTY QUICKLY.

MAYBE I SHOULD GET SOME FRESH AIR.

UGH, MAYBE JUST SIT OUT HERE FOR A WHILE. I DON'T WANT TO WALK ALL THE WAY DOWN.

I WONDER WHY THEY'RE CROUCHED DOWN LIKE THAT? ARE THEY HAVING A HARD TIME HEARING?

POLICE RESPONDING TO SEVERAL CALLS

SHOTS FIRED IN FLORIDA HIGH SCHOOL

PARKLAND SCHOOL LATEST IN US MASS SHOOTINGS

ONGOING ARREST AND EVACUATION

QUILL...

IS IT **THAT** PHONE CALL? THE "COME HOME" CALL?

I FEEL LIKE I'M WATCHING SOMETHING THAT I SHOULDN'T.

NO. QUILL WILL COME BACK TO CLASS.

I HAVE TO STOP THINKING LIKE THIS.

BUT QUILL DIDN'T COME BACK TO CLASS.

INSTEAD, THEIR ROOMMATE CAME AND GOT THEIR STUFF.

SORRY.

AND WHEN THEY DID, I FELT GUILTY.

LIKE I KNEW SOMETHING I SHOULDN'T.

QUILL, HOW'D THAT LAST COMIC COME OUT FOR YOU?

IT DIDN'T; I'VE BEEN GONE ALL WEEK.

MY SISTER WAS AT PARKLAND DURING THE SHOOTING.

OH MY GOD, IS SHE OK?

YEAH, SHE WASN'T HURT, JUST, YOU KNOW...

I'M SO SORRY, I THOUGHT, MAYBE--

YEAH, I THOUGHT OF YOU.

SINCE YOU DID THAT COMIC ABOUT THE SHOOTING YOU WERE IN.

217

OK, GUYS, LET'S START CLASS.

I WANTED TO HELP.

BUT I FELT GUILTY.

IT FELT LIKE I WAS PREYING ON THEM. I FELT DESPERATE TO CONNECT TO SOMEONE, ANYONE WHO COULD UNDERSTAND A FRACTION OF WHAT THESE THINGS DO TO PEOPLE.

AND IT'S NOT FAIR. I WANTED TO BE FRIENDS BEFORE ANY OF THIS HAPPENED.

BUT NOW I FEEL LIKE THAT WOULD BE WRONG.

BECAUSE I HAVE THESE ULTERIOR MOTIVES. SELFISH. I WANT TO BE UNDERSTOOD.

HEY, I JUST WANTED TO SEE IF YOU WERE OK.

YEAH, I AM.

SHE NEVER DID, BUT THAT'S OK. I DON'T THINK I WOULD HAVE, EITHER.

BZZT

JEEZ, WHAT IS MOM TAGGING ME IN THIS TIME? IT BETTER NOT BE ONE OF THOSE OLD-PEOPLE MEMES.

MARCH FOR OUR LIVES?

THE PARKLAND STUDENTS ARE PUTTING IT ON IN DC?

DC

MEET UP

CALANDER

I'LL HAVE TO CHECK IT OUT AS SOON AS I GET BACK TO THE APARTMENT.

OOPS!

HONK

GET OUT OF THE ROAD, YOU IDIOT!

THIS LOOKS GREAT!

I CAN GO TO THIS.

SAV →
DC

BOOK NOW

IT WAS TIME TO GO BACK TO DC.

WASHINGTON, DC

SAVANNAH

AND FACE SOME OF THOSE FEARS HEAD-ON.

BUT I WAS PRETTY RESTLESS ON THE WAY THERE.

IT JUST FELT DIFFERENT THIS TIME. LIKE SOMETHING WAS COMING TO A HEAD.

AND JOSH AND CHLOE WERE FLYING ALL THE WAY FROM ROSEBURG TO GO, TOO.

OK, ALL BUNDLED UP.

MAN, I WISH I COULD HAVE COME A COUPLE OF DAYS EARLY AND GONE TO SOME MUSEUMS.

CHLOE SAID THEY'D BE AROUND HERE SOMEWHERE.

I'LL JUST WAIT HERE, THEN.

HEY! KINDRA!

231

HEY, GUYS.

DO YOU MIND IF WE TAG ALONG?

SURE!

WHILE WE GATHERED IN THE STREETS, PRESIDENT TRUMP PLAYED GOLF.

HEY, GUYS, CHECK OUT THAT LADY'S SIGN.

I FELT LIKE I WAS WHERE I WAS SUPPOSED TO BE.

SERIOUSLY?

EXCUSE US!

SO MANY PEOPLE...

OK, MOVE PLEASE.

VOTE THEM OUT

#ENOUGH

I'M ABOUT TO LOSE IT. WHY ARE THEY ACTING LIKE THEY CAN'T BE BOTHERED?

THERE'S NO ROOM.

EXCUSE US.

JUST BREATHE.

SHE SAID THERE'S NO ROOM!

HEY! I SEE THE FENCE!

JUST A FEW MORE STEPS.

I'M GOING TO PUKE.

ARE YOU GUYS ALL RIGHT?

YEAH, WE JUST GOT A LITTLE OVERWHELMED IN THE CROWD.

HERE, JOSH, USE THIS.

THAT GUY IS MY HERO.

IT WAS SUPER QUICK FROM THERE.

I'M COMING DOWN FROM A PANIC ATTACK.

HE ALSO THREW UP.

OK, LET'S GET YOU ON ONE OF THE BEDS.

JOSH LOOKS PRETTY SICK.

MAYBE I SHOULD BE SEEING SOMEONE ABOUT THIS.

IT'S OK, SWEETIE, JUST HAVE A SEAT.

HI.

243

ARE YOU OK?

THERE'S A LOT OF PEOPLE.

SHE'S ALL RIGHT; SHE JUST GOT A LITTLE OVERWHELMED AND HAD TROUBLE BREATHING.

MY FRIENDS AND I HAD TO TAKE A BREAK, TOO.

SHE WAS DOING OK FOR A WHILE BUT WANTED A BREAK.

BUT WHEN WE TRIED TO MOVE TO A LESS CROWDED PLACE, PEOPLE WOULDN'T LET US THROUGH.

WHAT, SERIOUSLY? EVEN FOR A KID?

EVEN THOUGH WE TOLD THEM I COULDN'T BREATHE.

THAT'S NOT OK.

WELL, I THINK YOU'RE VERY BRAVE FOR COMING OUT AT ALL.

YES, SHE IS.

I THOUGHT I WAS GOING TO GET SOME CLOSURE FROM BEING HERE, BUT IT JUST MADE ME MORE UPSET.

I FELT STUPID FOR THINKING IT WAS GOING TO BE THIS BIG HEALING THING FOR ME.

HEY, JOSH IS FEELING A BIT BETTER. WE'RE GOING TO SEE IF WE CAN GET INTO THE MUSEUM SO WE CAN WATCH AND MAYBE FIND SOMEWHERE TO SIT.

SOUNDS GREAT. LET'S GO.

BYE!

246

WHILE WE WERE HEADING TO THE MUSEUM, I REMEMBER HEARING THE TAIL END OF A SPEECH BY ONE OF THE PARKLAND STUDENTS.

"THIS MARCH IS NOT THE CLIMAX.

"IT'S THE BEGINNING."

BUT I HAD CLASSES DURING SUMMER AND COULDN'T GO HOME, AND IT MADE ME FEEL AWFUL.

THE MARCH HAD INSPIRED ME TO DO SOMETHING ABOUT WHAT I WAS EXPERIENCING.

I WANTED TO DO SOMETHING, BUT I DIDN'T KNOW WHAT.

UNTIL I GOT CONTACTED BY SOMEONE WHO HAD SEEN A COMIC I HAD DONE ON THE SHOOTING.

SHE WAS PUTTING TOGETHER AN ANTHOLOGY OF SURVIVORS' STORIES AND WANTED ME TO PARTICIPATE.

IT FELT NICE THAT SOMEONE WANTED TO HEAR OUR STORIES.

AND IT GAVE ME AN IDEA ABOUT HOW I COULD USE MY VOICE.

SO I GOT
TO WORK.

ABSOLUTELY

SEND

BUT IT WAS A LOT MORE DIFFICULT THAN I THOUGHT.

IT WAS HARD TO OPEN UP.

SO I DECIDED TO JUST TOUCH UP THE COMIC THAT THEY'D SEEN.

I WONDER WHO WOULD EVEN WANT TO READ SOMETHING LIKE THAT?

WAIT, ME, ACTUALLY!

I EVEN WENT LOOKING FOR A BOOK ABOUT HOW TO DEAL WITH THE AFTERMATH OF A SHOOTING, BUT I COULDN'T FIND ONE.

MAYBE I COULD MAKE A BOOK TO SHOW PEOPLE LIKE ME THAT THEY AREN'T ALONE. OR THAT THEIR FEELINGS ARE NORMAL.

THE PROFESSORS KEEP SAYING, WRITE SOMETHING YOU WANT TO READ.

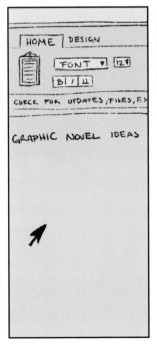

HOME | DESIGN

FONT ▼ | 12⁊

B | I | U

CHECK FOR UPDATES, FIXES, F.X

GRAPHIC NOVEL IDEAS

A CHANCE TO TELL MY STORY. WHAT WOULD THAT EVEN LOOK LIKE?

AS SUMMER ENDED, THERE WAS ANOTHER SHOOTING.

WHOA.

THERE WAS A SHOOTING IN JACKSONVILLE.

JACKSONVILLE? THAT'S NOT VERY FAR FROM HERE.

THERE'S A VIDEO.

WHAT?

IT'S AN AUDIO RECORDING FROM ONE OF THE STREAMERS.

STREAMERS?

IT WAS AT A VIDEO GAME CONVENTION.

.PLAYSTREAMLIVE@JACKSON mp3

JACKSONVILLE LIVE AN

LIVESTREAM . . .

LOADING . . .

HAHAHA, YEAH, MAN, THEY'RE PROBABLY WRAPPING UP THE TOURNAMENT.

WOW, HEY, DID THAT SOUND REAL? THOSE PEOPLE ARE RUNNING.

GET DOWN! GET DOWN! WHAT'S HAPPENING?

N SHOOTIN CONVENT

N JACKSONVI LATEST A PUBLIC DI

I KNOW I SHOULD GO IN, BUT THEY'RE ALWAYS BOOKED, AND SOMEONE ELSE MIGHT REALLY NEED IT.

BUT I'M CLEARLY NOT GOOD AT TELLING WHEN I NEED HELP. AND THE THIRD ANNIVERSARY IS ALMOST HERE.

I HAVE TO DO THIS.

THERE'S NOTHING WRONG WITH THIS.

UM, COUNSELING?

RIGHT DOWN THIS HALL, HONEY.

THANKS.

STUDENT COUNSELING

HI, UM, I WAS WONDERING IF I COULD SIGN UP FOR COUNSELING?

UNFORTUNATELY, WE'RE ALL BOOKED FOR THE TERM, UNLESS, OF COURSE, IT'S AN EMERGENCY.

OH, NO. IT'S OK. I CAN WAIT.

HERE...I CAN PUT YOU ON THE WAITING LIST IN CASE WE HAVE CANCELLATIONS.

AND HERE'S A LIST OF DOCTORS IN THE CITY IF YOU NEED HELP BEFORE WE CAN GET YOU IN.

I REALLY CAN'T AFFORD A DOCTOR, BUT THANKS, I'LL LOOK INTO IT.

THANK YOU.

I KNOW PEOPLE THINK THAT RAIN IS SAD, BUT IT ALWAYS FEELS LIKE IT'S A FRESH START. LIKE IT WASHES AWAY ALL THE BAD SO YOU CAN START OVER.

HI, SORRY, EXCUSE ME.

SORRY, I'M A COUNSELOR, AND I JUST WANTED TO ASK IF YOU HAPPEN TO BE AN INTERNATIONAL STUDENT?

WE HAVE TO MAKE ROOM FOR YOU IF YOU ARE.

OH, NO, I'M NOT.

IT MIGHT HAVE JUST BEEN A PART OF HER JOB--

BUT IT MEANT EVERYTHING TO ME THAT SHE FOLLOWED ME DOWN THE STREET JUST TO CHECK.

OK, WELL, JUST HANG ON A LITTLE LONGER. WE GET A LOT OF CANCELLATIONS, SO WE SHOULD GET YOU IN SOON.

THANK YOU SO MUCH.

JUST A LITTLE LONGER. I CAN DO THIS JUST A LITTLE WHILE LONGER.

IT FELT BETTER KNOWING THAT I'D BE GETTING HELP SOON, THAT I WOULDN'T HAVE TO DO THIS ALONE.

AND WORKING ON THE BOOK HURT A LITTLE, BUT IT WAS HELPING ME FIGURE OUT MY FEELINGS.

BUT SHOOTINGS JUST KEPT HAPPENING.

THOUSAND OAKS WAS EVERY SURVIVOR'S WORST NIGHTMARE, BECAUSE A SURVIVOR FROM THE LAS VEGAS SHOOTING WAS KILLED IN ANOTHER.

I CAN'T TAKE IT ANYMORE. A YEAR. HE ESCAPED A SHOOTING AND WAS KILLED IN ANOTHER A YEAR LATER, MOM.

I KNOW I'M FREAKING OUT, BUT AM I CRAZY?

I JUST DON'T FEEL SAFE!

AND I FEEL TERRIBLE FOR BEING UPSET, BECAUSE I'M NOT EVEN THE ONE BEING AFFECTED. THEY LOST PEOPLE THEY LOVED TONIGHT.

IT'S JUST GETTING WORSE. I DON'T FEEL--I'M NOT WELL.

I STARTED SHARING MY BOOK IDEA WITH MY CLASS.

MOST PEOPLE WERE SUPPORTIVE.

AND IT FELT GOOD TO BE OPEN ABOUT WHAT WAS GOING ON.

WHICH IS WORSE WHEN YOU'RE THE ONE WHO BRINGS IT UP.

RIGHT! IT'S LIKE THEY DIDN'T EVEN HEAR YOU.

THEY DON'T HAVE TO SAY ANYTHING SUPER BRILLIANT THAT'LL FIX THE PROBLEM.

BUT DON'T PRETEND LIKE I DIDN'T SAY ANYTHING JUST BECAUSE YOU'RE UNCOMFORTABLE IN THE MOMENT.

AS UNCOMFORTABLE AS THEY ARE HEARING IT, THAT'S ONLY A FRACTION OF HOW UNCOMFORTABLE I AM ALL THE TIME CARRYING IT AROUND.

I WAS PROUD THAT I TALKED ABOUT IT.

IT FELT LIKE I WAS WORKING TO GET BETTER.

THERE WERE STILL BAD DAYS--

BUT IT WAS A LITTLE EASIER TO CALM MYSELF DOWN.

WHEN I SAW EMERGENCY RESPONSE RIGHT OUTSIDE MY BUILDING ONE DAY--

I THOUGHT THE WORST HAD HAPPENED. I THOUGHT A SHOOTING HAD HAPPENED.

MY HEAD WAS IMMEDIATELY FILLED WITH WHAT-IFS:

WHAT IF MY PROFESSORS WERE KILLED?

WHAT IF PEOPLE TRIED TO RUN BUT DIDN'T MAKE IT PAST THE HALL?

BUT I TOOK A BREATH.

AND IT DIDN'T STOP THE THOUGHTS COMPLETELY--

BUT I WAS ABLE TO STOP THE PANIC ATTACK.

IT TURNED OUT THEY WERE THERE BECAUSE A WINDOW HAD BEEN BROKEN ACROSS THE STREET.

I WAS STILL SCARED, BUT I FELT LIKE I COULD PUSH MYSELF AND GO INSIDE AND DO WORK.

I DON'T THINK I COULD HAVE DONE THAT A FEW WEEKS EARLIER.

IT'S OK TO BE SCARED. ACKNOWLEDGE ITS EFFECT AND THAT IT'S THERE--

AND SAY THIS IS A BATTLE WORTH WAGING.

IT WAS DIFFICULT, BUT I FOUND THAT MAKING THE CHOICE WAS THE HARDEST PART.

HAVE U SEEN THIS? link.xzr

ONCE I WAS DOING THE THING THAT SCARED ME, IT WAS USUALLY A LOT EASIER.

WHAT'S THIS? AN NRA VIDEO?

SAY, "HOW DARE YOU STAND ON THE GRAVES OF THESE CHILDREN AND PUT FORTH YOUR POLITICAL AGENDA?" JUST SHAME THEM OF THE WHOLE THING.

IT WAS A VIDEO OF NRA OFFICIALS INSTRUCTING A GROUP FROM NEW ZEALAND ON HOW TO SPIN SCHOOL SHOOTINGS IF THERE WAS ONE THERE.

BY EXPLOITING THE SURVIVORS, BY DOING THE VERY THING THEY WERE ACCUSING OTHERS OF DOING.

WE SHOULD BE THE ONES TELLING THE STORY AND LEADING THE TALKS.

I RETURNED TO ROSEBURG WITH A DEDICATION TO GETTING BETTER--

AND TO BEING HONEST WITH MY FRIENDS AND FAMILY ABOUT WHAT I WENT THROUGH.

I SPOKE UP MORE ABOUT HOW I FELT.

I TOLD JASMINE ABOUT WHAT HAPPENED IN THE GARAGE.

I'M SO SORRY I KEPT IT FROM YOU.

I'M JUST SO GLAD I CALLED!

281

KNOCK
KNOCK

HEY, MOM, WHAT'S UP?

HEY, THEY CANCELED THE CHARITY RUN THIS YEAR.

I GUESS THEY DIDN'T HAVE ENOUGH VOLUNTEERS.

OH REALLY?

SOME PEOPLE DECIDED TO RUN IN THE PARK TOGETHER ANYWAY. BUT I VISITED THE SCHOOL BRIEFLY.

EXIT
UCC
STATE POLICE

I JUST NEEDED TO SEE THAT IT WAS SAFE AND SOUND.

WE DON'T HAVE CONTROL IF BAD THINGS HAPPEN TO US OR THOSE WE LOVE.

BUT WE CAN CHOOSE WHAT TO DO WITH OURSELVES AFTER THEY HAPPEN.

IT'S A JOURNEY WE GO THROUGH TOGETHER.

FOR AS DIFFICULT AS IT IS TO LISTEN, IT IS EQUALLY DIFFICULT FOR THE PERSON SHARING.

I THINK EVERYONE WANTS TO BE HEARD AND HAS A STORY WORTH SHARING.

AND THE LAST THING THAT SHOULD KEEP US SILENT OR FROM LISTENING IS ONE ANOTHER.

AUTHOR'S NOTE

I'd like to share one more moment with you. A good portion of people who have wanted or attempted to take their lives say that they are glad they didn't. When I first heard this, it almost made me feel even more miserable, because I thought that this feeling would come at major achievements in my life: graduation or a friend's wedding or getting a book deal. I would spend most of these important milestones pacing around and waiting for this euphoric joy I was supposed to feel, and when I didn't, I would be disappointed. I felt a lot of shame for several years for being indifferent toward being alive and for those times when I still struggled with those thoughts.

So here's the moment, about four years after my attempt, when I was truly happy that I was still on this earth. Jasmine has moved down to LA for her work, and I am visiting. This is in the weeks leading up to the pandemic, late January of 2020. Her husband takes me out to go surfing with one of his buddies. They decide to take me the day after it has rained, so the water is all murky and gray from runoff from the city, and it's frigid. I've been surfing a few times, but never in cold water. We've been out there for an hour or so, and I'm not able to stand up on the board. I keep getting tossed under the freezing waves over and over again. I paddle out. I grab a wave. I start to stand. I'm under. Over and over. But there's just something about the moment that the water takes me under. I relax and let it flip me around, and it puts me on my feet. I stick the landing, so to speak, and just walk out of the surf. Eventually, I'm so tired that Jasmine's husband and his friend have to help me get back out over the surf so that I can keep going, but I'm not even trying to stand anymore. I'm just waiting for that moment when the water takes me under.

I get time to myself when the boys are a little way off. I'm sitting out on my board, letting the waves go by, resting, and it hits then. I start crying. Hard. It's not euphoric joy. It's gratitude. Unbelievable, overwhelming gratitude. I could try to intellectualize that moment. I could say something to the effect that the waves were a metaphor for letting go of control, or that water is often symbolic of emotions, but I truly think I was just enjoying myself. It was fun being alive. I liked crashing into the waves. I liked getting tossed around. I liked that it was freezing cold and kind of stinky and a little bit slimy. Most of all, I liked that I kept doing something just because I wanted to.

I've had several more moments like that since then. They're not frequent, and often they're in circumstances that I don't imagine would appeal to many others. The best thing about having them is that when I feel myself struggling again, I can think about them. I'm not worried about having another one of these moments of gratitude. I'm comforted knowing that I have the potential to feel the most alive while playing in dirty water.

RESOURCES

THE REBELS PROJECT

Website: *therebelsproject.org*

Founded by survivors of the Columbine shooting, this supportive group has worked to create a safe environment, specific resources, and programs to help survivors heal. Involvement can also include donation, sponsorship, and volunteer service.

I highly encourage anyone that is a part of the survivor community to reach out and take advantage of the thoughtful and much-needed resources this group provides.

NATIONAL SUICIDE PREVENTION LIFELINE

Website: *suicidepreventionlifeline.org*

Phone: 1-800-273-8255

Available 24/7, they connect you with the nearest crisis center. Their website also includes education on warning signs, prevention, and other topics surrounding suicide attempts.

MARCH FOR OUR LIVES

Website: *marchforourlives.com*

Gun violence is not random, and March For Our Lives has numerous programs, events, and resources available to educate on and help combat this issue. Covering issues like mass shootings, police brutality, domestic violence, and hate crimes, this organization is empowering others to vote on policies that save lives.

You can join a local chapter, donate, or support through merch and awareness.

ACKNOWLEDGMENTS

I forgot to thank my mom in a graduation speech in 2016, and she hasn't let me live it down since. So I'd first like to thank my mom for all her support, not only during the making of this book, but in all the events that led up to it and after. I'd also like to thank my aunt Angie and uncle Scott for being incredibly encouraging and supportive of my art education and career.

I have a number of teachers and professors in my life who helped set me on my way. I'd like to thank the entire staff of Umpqua Community College for the absolute best educational experience of my life. Special thanks to the art department, and especially Susan Rochester. I would not have pursued art without you.

Thank you to the professors and staff of the Sequential Art Department at SCAD. You literally made this possible.

Thank you to everyone at Little, Brown who helped shape this book and gave it a place to grow. Thank you to my amazing editor, Andrea Colvin, and art director, Megan McLaughlin. Thank you to Juan Murillo for your amazing work during the coloring.

Lastly, thank you to Jasmine. You and Lexa are the reason I'm here today.

ABOUT THE AUTHOR

Chloe Friedlein

KINDRA NEELY is an artist and writer based in southern Oregon. She took her first drawing class, Drawing Nature, at UCC and still likes to regularly hike the trails to sketch flowers and ferns. *Numb to This* is her debut graphic novel.